Mathematics in Color

by

Joseph J. Kozma

1-28-09
For Amy
Hope you enjoy
this little volume
with best wishes

Indian Paintbrush Poets

Published by Indian Paintbrush Poets, an imprint of
Pearn and Associates, Inc., Boulder, Colorado.
For information about our products and services
please contact us at happypoet@hotmail.com,
(720) 620-4499.

Cover design by Anne Kilgore.

Acknowledgements

Many lives crossed my paths. Many walked with me,
some just passed by. They gave me insight and
determination. I thank them all. Special thanks for
Victor Pearn of Pearn and Associates for his advice
and encouragement.

Library of Congress Control Number: 2009926083

Kozma, Joseph J. 1924
Mathematics in Color, by Joseph J. Kozma. First Edition.
ISBN 978-0-9777318-8-6 paper.

Contents

Love

Pages of War

Ninetoro's Pages

Darkness

Prayers

Life

Introduction

This book started years ago. Many poems saw the light, and hoped for a future. It never happened. Through fate, and misfortune only one poem survived, and fossilized over the years. Its title is the title of this book commemorating a time that was, meaning existed. After many empty years this book looks back and asks *Mathematics in Color* to lead on . . . .

Joseph J. Kozma

Mathematics in Color

Yesterday's waters did not see me swimming,
tomorrow there will be no bubbles,
so I have to die today.

Five and ten and more and more
fists are raised to heaven.
Clouds are sunshine
and sunshine is earth.
The earth is warm as never before.
It never will be like today
and a month ago and nowhere in time.

My fingers cross each other deep in the earth.
They will never forget.
One, two, one-two, one-two.
Why the silence?
One-two, one-two, one-two,
this is the answer.

The circulation stops just for two seconds.
Cynics say, "who cares."
Priests throw fire crosses across the chapels,
bedrooms and closets.
Down, in the street, heated cell complexes are
still fainting. One after another.
They enjoy it.

One, two, one-two, one-two?
One-two, one-two, one-two.

How many seconds alive?
How silent is the silence?
Fluctuating, vibrating, falling and questioning
silence.
Here and there.
Now and now and just one more now.

It was yesterday.
The waters are dust today.
Evenly, madly, firmly loosened dust.
Way, way back.
Creatures crawl creeping.
Birds, bombs and gods recreate heirs
for the vanishing waters.
We do not see them.

One and two, one and two
simple, real, beautiful rhythm of today.
Let us stop the time.

Love

Timeless Love

Time has come again
looking for an answer.
Perhaps an action,
perhaps a deed,
more and more
an accomplishment perhaps.
Above all that is my love.
Love is timeless.

The Start

The shadows of the heat
were dancing on the pavement.
You looked at me just once
and a new world began,
this time with you in it.

You and I

What do the stars think behind the clouds?
What do the clouds think of the stars?
What does the rainbow think of the ocean?
What does the ocean think of the rainbow?

The breath is heavy
while the darkness
soft-shoes the road
and hides the star-dome.

Your hair is wavy
when the sunshine's
silken fingers comb the wheat fields
kissing rainbows
into raindrops.

Do the stars behind the clouds know
that the rainbows will come tomorrow?
Can the eyes of a gazing ocean
see the raindrops melt to beauty?

Can just for a moment
be everything clear?
Today as clear as tomorrow
and tomorrow clearer than yesterday.

Can just for one moment
your eyes be mine
and my blood yours?

Can just for one moment
be nothing else,
just you and I,
just the two of us?

Love Arrived

Love arrived on golden wings
in the heat of a golden day.
A message as clear as a comet's path
and as rare, plotted for
a thousand years, destined to
leave the universe and settle.
Here it was with no boundaries,
Fatefully glorious and humbly true.
It perfused us. We were helpless.
Our hearts synchronized. Love arrived.

Here We Are

It was there when it began.
In the darkness, in the space,
there it was.

Then the light came,
there was no more.

Then somewhere, sometime
after the oceans,
after the heavens,
after the creatures,
there it was.

And I knew, I felt
over and over and over:
there was love, love to be
and love to stay.

Here we are now, without time,
without sunsets, without darkness.
Just us. Here we are.

Our Road in Time

Are the stars still piercing the night?
Does the darkness invite the day?
Are you still on the road with me,
where nobody else goes
just you and I?
Look, the pavement shimmers
like when we built it.
Part of it gold, part of it timeless.
Solid, you see no tracks, no ruts
just a view back and ahead.
See, the road still takes us,
just takes us.

Dream

The moon looked down
and turned the lake milky.
Just then, I started to ache for you.
I saw your face and the face of love
in the milky lake, I saw it well.

Then you kissed me.
From the lake came
not a wave, not a ripple,
just your kiss, your passion, your life.

The night hurried toward
the sunrise, smoothly guarding
a secret. I held you until the light
took over. Then the lake reclaimed you.

Sketch of a Day

The day went like a freight train.
Heated rails sparkled,
the earth rumbled.
It slowed down and
took on speed in
a rhythm unpredictable.
Hours suffered under
the weight ever increasing.
Merciless grind, raw intrusion into
virgin territory of
color and love,
lasting too long.
When the tail light
glared, laughing, the offense
subsided. There was
Eden. There were you.

The Inerasable

Can you erase the nights
of ecstasy? Can you stop
the rhythm of our hearts
synchronizing without effort.
Can you stop remembering?

We never planned the steps
that took us by surprise.
Sweet and strong was the taste
that took us higher than high,
right up to the stars.

Strong was the cover that kept
us protected. We had a shelter
solid and safe, impenetrable.
It lasted and lasted.
Can you erase that?

The Search

I loved you here and beyond the
tundra, the steppes, the oceans,
the deserts, the icebergs and
beyond any nook on this earth;
and you left me loving you.

Where are you now? I know you
left my love here to linger,
to freeze and stiffen, depart from
me to wander alone to where
nobody goes only the ones who search.

Will it ever find you?
Will it ever find you?

Pages of War

Blood and History

From fine trickle
to mighty stream
the blood was allowed to flow.
It came from hearts
and brains and guts.
Bones and pores
opened up to see the
daylight real and throbbing.
Swords searched and
found and served up
blood over and over
as a proof of victory.
The flow of blood had
no limitation.
Bullets punctured sheets
of armor and sheets of skin.
Big spectacle for major
players, for great gamblers
of history.

Silence

The sun porch was my shelter.
Bare walls and a glass ceiling
shielded me and I believed.
The concrete was cold on my chest
as I lay there, looking up, waiting
for the glass to shatter under
the bombs. The concrete is
cold when your heart is racing
and your skin is trying to hide.
I took comfort and hoped in a split
second warning before I died.

There was no warning, no death,
just thundering rumble of
undulating air under waves
of motors on wings. Devastation.
Then silence like before creation.
Silence.

Hungarian Teamster on the Russian Front

You were whistling,
the horses were pissing,
there was peace on Earth.
Then you went to war.

You spent the days,
you spent the nights among bullets and smoke.
You survived. Killing
cold whitened your toes.
The eastern lager taught
you to curse and hate,
purified you and corrupted your thoughts,
weighed heavily on you.
You survived.
Year and a half and
you are here.
Your horses, you did not know,
followed you and lived
a while. Famine almost killed
them. Soldiers' starvation
got to them first.
Soldiers starve in war at times.
They starve in fight,
starve in camps, starve
in body and spirit.
You survived fight,
hell and starvation.
You are at home,
you can whistle again.

War Never Ending

The Ratas ground coffee
in the sky.
The Messerschmitts ripped the
air to shreds.
A war was on.

New graves opened
waiting for occupants.
Fire and smoke crept in.
A war was on.

Fingers pointed to the sky.
Fingers pointed to Berlin and Moscow.
Fingers soon died.
A war was on.

The war just kept on going.
The air remained thick.
The sky still had songbirds and vultures.
The war just refused to end.

My Company in the Sky

On a road in Bavaria
I walked for survival.
Total isolation, nobody around
just the wind, birds and trees,
futility all around in time.
Death with no resurrection.
Wishes and hopes circling like magic
to make my feet master the miles.
The vast abandoned landscape
made me feel lonely.
Silence like nirvana lasted a while,
then switched to a roar up in the sky.
Two hundred liberators broke up the silence.
Magnificent sight, magnificent sound.
My legs felt regenerated. The landscape
was still abandoned, futile and barren,
but I was not alone.

Looking for Heaven

Dark, heated clouds
hovered over us
looking for an answer
when there was no question.

And the bombs fell,
the cannons roared,
blood filled the cracks
in walls and pavements.

Is there an earth without a heaven?
Is there a desert without a sea?
Is there a cloud without a heart?
The questions came, late, but came.

The cannons kept roaring,
the blood never stopped.
Muscles went limp
and the sky split open.

We looked up in fear.
We looked up in hope.
We stood and trembled.
There was no heaven.

Dolores Inferni

The truck was grinding
on the road, fueled by
wood-bricks-generated
gas, as smoothly as a
well oiled machine gun.

Sitting in the truck's open bed,
shielding our eyes from the cold
spring-wind and the
slanting sun
we watched those who slept
along the roadside.

Others were walking
without sight, just following,
just simply following a
line, from where we were,
without a beginning and
without a destination,
except for one goal to
stay alive a little longer.

The ones who slept
would never wake up.
We did not know that.

A Sight in Motion

I saw the dust that
was a house a minute ago.
I saw the torso that had
legs before I left the
shelter. It all looked
so natural. Quick change,
destruction, no regrets.

I saw a halo above all
that, structured to justify
killing after killing. There
was no focus, just organized
senselessness devoid of
form with lack of credibility.

I felt the air, the world really,
adhering to me, dragging
me toward where I did
not want to be. I stood
firm with my feet planted.
Then the halo departed.

Ninetoro's Pages

Ninetoro's Christmas

If Mary could make it,
if Joseph could make it,
if Jesus could make it,
then he, the elder, also could make it.

He never had a son, or a daughter.
He was older than they would have been.
He was drinking from a cup, cold
and bitter, signaling the future.

A white flag was on his mind.
He could wave it any time.
He waited for a kiss instead, he
was Ninetoro in the crowd on the hill.

Ninetoro's Delight

Ninetoro saw a snail
soaring with an eagle.
What a pair,
what a sight,
Ninetoro was delighted.

Ninetoro Fainted

The hillside under Ninetoro's
feet moved slowly toward
the open range of a thousand cows.
He felt the strange movement of
the earth, frozen into a slanted existence.
His feet were sinking. He looked
but he could not see what
he felt. It was simply absurd.

Absurdity, born just then,
asked him to declare to
the pasture below that
beef was all right to eat,
that cholesterol was just a crystal
shaped like flakes with sharp
cutting edges but harmless, sneaking
through the tight passes in his arteries.

He had an urge to count the cows
grazing as if nothing was happening.
He did not do it. Instead
he visualized the jungle of branches
of his arteries, the walls,
the plaques, the hesitant flow of blood
in some delicately tight spots.
He felt the hillside moving. He fainted.

The Immersion of Ninetoro

Ninetoro looked at the
restless mirror that moved
from horizon to horizon.
It shook, undulated, changed
color from dark green
to silver, crested and
ebbed, hushed to a silence
hardly audible, then burst
to thunderous ovation and shatter.

Where does this all come
from, he read his eyes
looking inward. Within
him questions burst into
flames. With burning
eyes he deciphered them.
He stood there stone stiff
his feet deep in the sand,
eyes fixed inside and out.

Fixed eyes see the most.
There is no break, no fence
no separation, just one
unit. It melted through
him, united him with
millions of years and
that many answers. He knew
how to sort them, how to
feel them. He immersed.

Cervantes and Ninetoro's Shoes

When reading Cervantes
Ninetoro could not help
polishing his shoes.
It was a must. A drive
threatening his sanity.
He knew it, he was
almost proud of it.
He wondered who
other than Cervantes was
interested in his shoes.

Ninetoro

He was born to turn one day
into a great artist.
He stepped into the world
with a brush in his hand.
His eyes saw shapes and colors
both ways, from the inside
outward and inward from the outside.
His paintings lived, he put
life on canvas trimmed with
suspended animation with
a depth never seen before.
He never slept without one eye
open. He saw two worlds,
one behind the eyelids and one
ahead without limits. He saw
the uniqueness of shapes and
the depth of colors. They had a
meaning on and off canvas.
He was Ninetoro.

Confusion of Ninetoro

His thoughts faded into the distance,
they got close to the setting sun,
suddenly the night began.

Ninetoro was wondering. He lived
with his thoughts, bright and airy.
They caressed everything his eyes could see.

He knew how to keep them formed.
No treasure, no tragedy, no magnificence
of a landscape distracted him.

Yet, the night caught him by surprise.
No announcement, no warning, just there.
He tried to understand the sudden change.

To him only one unit existed
with phases and smooth transitions.
Ninetoro was thrown off balance.

Prayer of Ninetoro

Ninetoro looked at the river
and the buildings beyond.
White walls broke into the
landscape of foggy dreams
grown into leaves on
branches made of twisted air.
All that he felt. Inside,
he stored unending rows
of years marching by.
Ninetoro started to pray.
He did not know nor guess
where the words came from.
He never talked to the
Lord before. He never prayed.
Now his heart, his breath,
his skin, his being urged him on.
He closed his eyes and
thanked to the Lord for
listening to him. The
river and the walls vanished.

The Loss of Ninetoro

Ninetoro's pockets were empty.
His fingers remembered well
the weight of gold. Ninetoro
lost it all.

There was a time when
sorting gold in its million
forms came before love
and song.

He felt an emptiness crawling
around his heart, in his skin, in his being,
he remembered.

He looked and saw little.
He crumbled the air
with his fingers dry and cold,
he lost it all.

Ninetoro's Vision

There was something
strange in Ninetoro's gaze, perhaps
something wrong, even.
He was expecting a different
vision, he was surprised.
He looked almost frightened.
A slight shake of his head
told about a tension he felt
in his heart. "Not now" he
whispered. He wanted to shout
"Stop, stop for awhile,
stop for years, just stop."
He turned away, his eyes met
full colors, bright and soothing.
Small flames danced on the
ground, scents riding on
petals of blooms just begotten
floated and moved in
a pomp never seen before.
He turned back, far, far away
Ninetoro saw a coffin rolling
toward him. Then the vision faded,
the hallucination ended.

Darkness

Away

Something between daylight
and darkness sits on my chest,
cries in uncontrollable despair.
My arms are crossing to lift me
above the clouds, a bundle
trying to escape where
twilight reigns without fear,
where there is no past and
there is no future, where
there is no reason to cry.

Hallelujah

Your memory is not completely
erased, I am working on it now.
The stars are not blinking at
me, there is no perfume in the air.
You stomped out your meteoric
life, you left no footprints.
You built a road without return.
Looking back is futile, what you lost,
you lost, possibly everything. Your
memory fades as time assists
with your departure. When the
ribbon of the road turn into
a thread there will be nothing more.
I'll say hallelujah.

To a Feeling Almost Lost

Feeling, don't leave me now.
You are far but still visible.
Stay within sight
so you can return.

Something keeps me from
opening my arms to embrace
you. Something fights me
and keeps me from calling you back.

Yet, I know that without
feelings no color is seen,
no music is heard. Silence
and darkness, hand in hand, rule.

Though distant you are now,
you know you'll be back.
Better and fuller than ever.
We'll unite, we'll live again.

Deception Discovered

You listened to the wind.
It took you over desert so hot
that your skin, red and dry,
never recovered, you lost your happiness.
The wind betrayed you.
You realized too late
that you lost everything.
You only had one possession, guilt.

You listened to the river wide,
rushing, glistening and smiling.
You could not swim, as you know,
but you tried. The eddies
surrounded you. Happy, you thought
you were. Uproar and shame
derailed you. Your lungs lacked
air and substance. You felt only misery.

You listened to the thunder promising
convulsive elation with every word.
You hoped and believed.
Muddy, cold, evasive and crude
was the ground kissed by the thunder.
You hoped to partake but you
sunk deeply into inertia.
Muddy, hopeless and shamefully naked you were.

You knew then, it is better
to listen and plan than to be
picked up by crude forces
and perverted emotions

riding wild around you,
filling you with false hope
and choke you to silence,
force you to give it all up and be gone.

A House Without Walls

The house lost its walls,
there is no roof,
there are no floors,
just the windows remain.

A force multiphasic,
duplicating and quickly
gaining room where
no motion is possible.

I question the windows.
Is there a space without walls?
Are you guarding the senseless?
Are you something called sense?

A house without walls,
vanished roof, open windows,
is a concept with no parallel.
I live in that house.

Looking Back

I stepped in the soft space,
left stones, bricks and concrete behind.
I moved over sand, over water
feeling a fulfillment, detachment,
way, way above everything.
I was carried, pampered by
never seen or felt clarity of purpose.
I looked back. You watched
me from the balcony. I waved
to you to join me, to share
the impossible, the improbable.
You did not move. A bolt
of even greater clarity told me
all about us, it described us:
in all our years you never left the balcony.

Your Domain

Remember your garden with
colors never ending,
with soil of velvet and
air clear, soft and
wildly invigorating? Remember?

You were the center.
Your domain lived around you.
Why is it wilting now?
Your garden is collapsing.
You are depressed. You were the
spirit, the source, the fountain. You let it go.

Gardens are rebellious
you must know. You must
live in them, inhale their
spirit and breathe out
their essence to embellish
them. You failed. You
let the colors, the spirit,
the growth, the abundance,
the domain go. Now it is over.

Lies and Deceit

Lies and deceit where do you come from?
You hover over me at night,
chase me during the day,
paint my walls your colors.

You want me to live the way I can't.
You want to choke me,
you want to stab me,
so you can laugh.

What a pair you are.

Love How Far Did You Go?

Love, how far did you go?
Miles in one dimension, years in time.
Dissolved in the universe.

Love never to be found again,
never alive, so it seems,
never breathing, never gasping,
never here.

How far did you go love?
Can you be captured,
tamed, boosted and shored up?
A sign, just one, would do.

To Sisyphus

Our paths have crossed again, Sisyphus.
Hades is everywhere.
You left your stone with me
as you escaped. For months now
I have rolled your stone
to the top and again and again,
it rolled to my lap,
crushing my body and soul.
Is there a way to recover?
Can pieces be made whole?
Is there a second life?
Time flies on slow wings
to hurt. Move the stone
Sisyphus. Move the stone.
Take it back, take it back.

Slaves and Memories

Turn away from jaded memories
embellished, gold-plated and fabricated.
They are no substitute for reality,
they can exist only because of you.
Memories are made by you,
you shape them, you mold them
they are your slaves.
Slaves are to please you.
They work for you, the more
you have the more
you feel safe. Next, they betray you,
then they revolt.
Get rid of your slaves,
liberate them, turn them loose,
make yourself free.

Dream, More Dream

Your loving me was a dream,
but, as you know
dreams don't last.
Your love, if it ever lived
died awhile ago.
I did not know it.
O, how I know it now.
Is it too late, did the
dream last too long,
with no chance for more?
There is more with pain,
there is more with misery.
These are the shadows
in a dream. Sunshine
can help now.
Please sunshine, help.
Dream, O dream,
don't leave me now.
Not now, never.

Circle of Love, Broken

Is the time ever right
for a line to turn
into a circle?
A force liberating
the line, molding it
into a form when
the call arrives?
From its cavern of mystery
love surfaces and binds
circles around hearts, tight,
with an aim to be final.
But the circles break
at times. Jagged lines just
float, just float and float.

Birth of a Mirage

On the horizon, visible daily,
there was a happy site.
It was an inspiration,
it was a fountain,
it was a gem.
It was the staple, the energy,
the source. You etched deep longings
in my heart, made me
lean on you, we united.
Never a day without you.
Salvoes of triumphant bursts
of happiness lifted me
to levitate. You flourished
on the horizon, with no blemish,
no sorrow. Years of living flame,
years of exponential creations.
No brakes, just aims higher
than adulation, higher than
veneration, just your image growing.
One day your image thinned
you were still there, still visible
but with no message, no more to utter,
no more to show.
You looked away, turned into
a mirage. Untouchable,
visible without a structure.
Just a sight, just a sight,
nothing more.

Remorse

O remorse, O remorse,
how I hoped to meet you.
I wanted to idolize you,
make you a person,
respect you, caress you,
invite you to my bed,
make love to you.
But remorse, you remained
a stranger, unmoved,
cold eyes and frigid.
You never learned to live.
Then you vanished.

Goodbye

You said goodbye
months ago, without a word
without a sound.
I say goodbye now
because this is real.
Reality took you away.

It hurt for months to
see you gone, looking at me with
daily goodbyes,
senseless and painful.
You gambled, it did not work.
Goodbye should be
final, but it never
will be. It never will be.

November

Standing, looking out,
counting the leaves.
Why the torture,
why the counting?
Because fall will
take you before winter.
When the last leaf falls
you'll be gone.

Could a few leaves
winter on the branches?
Could you stay until
spring? We could count
the green leaves, we could
hope for summer.
In the meantime
the leaves keep on
falling, falling and falling,
It is November.

Child of the Night

You made the sunshine
sink away
and brought on the night.
Thick and cold,
the darkness prevails.
Our bones harden
as our skin shivers.
Why did you do it?
Senseless and empty
is our life now. Gone are the days,
there is no sunrise,
only the night
without mercy.
Meaningless future greets us
daily, frozen and mean.
Our feet slip
on the frozen ground,
on the ground nursed
by the darkness.
Some day, perhaps some day
a little light will be born,
a child of the night.

Prayers

Prayer

We are too late
for everything,
at times we are even
born too late.
If we are born only to die
O Lord O Lord
just let us be late.

Prayers to Soar Again

The temples are ready now,
steeples point to the sky.
Cold are the temples.
Frosty, wingless prayers
float around aimlessly
nowhere to go, never to be heard.
Prayers don't soar anymore.

No bushes are burning
to give prayers their wings.
Flare up again, oh burning bush,
make prayers soar, just make them soar.

Open Heart Surgery

Lord, you saw me
stretched out and lifeless
among lights and wires,
without a beating heart.

Your pity sustained me
your power diffused me,
life returned as if it had never left,
as if it just played a part.

Now points meet points,
see each other like before,
teaming up to lift and provide
beauty and strength for another stretch.

A Turnable Cheek

Lord, don't ask me to
turn the other cheek.
I have been stepped on,
kicked and made faceless,
I don't have another cheek
to turn.
Maybe a mask, Lord, maybe a mask
would give the illusion of
a turnable cheek.
A mask can pretend,
a fake cheek can turn
and your will be done.
Please, let me turn
the cheek of the mask.

Not Good at All

This is not good, Lord.
What are we going to do?
The sun comes up,
the sun goes down,
the earth rotates, the leaves fall
when they do.
Dreams pop up every night
by the millions
around the globe.
Petals shine and fade.
Ovens bake bread,
atoms play within molecules,
everything is in motion.
I am not in all this,
I am not. Where am I
Lord, where am I?
This is just not good.

A Request

If this is my lot, O Lord
so be it.
If this is to be my future too
so be it.
You started it all,
in your hands
rests the end.
After all of this pain
and hurt and suffering
sweeten the rest O Lord,
sweeten the rest.

Wishing and Begging

Enlighten me, Lord, enlighten me.
Cover me and inebriate me.
Give me clues, wailed or solid,
soft and hard,
with a secret code even,
just enlighten me.

Ease my pain, Lord, ease my pain.
Teach me to see, teach me to hear.
Unify my senses make me one.
Immerse me in what is, what has been
and what will be. Be close, be aloof
just ease my pain.

Select me to be a seer.
Train me to make discoveries,
truths uncamouflaged and real.
Give me a track or a highway,
tame the chaos around me
just select me, just select me.

Lord Say Yes

All the priests around the world,
clergymen and prophets
know well where the Lord resides,
they know how to keep a secret.

Reveal yourself, Lord, again
on the top and on the water.
Reveal your face eye to eye
let us see you first hand.

Let the trees grow with message anew,
let us read the lines.
Let us be part of you again,
clear the way, Lord, say yes.

Asking to be Heard

Talking to you is not easy.
You hear the bells of every cathedral,
hear the cannons of wars old and new,
prayers of the lost and revived,
rolling trains and sinking vessels,
expressions of a polished sun
and now my voice searching a way.
All that you do right now
in very real time,
following every change in every unit
of time without end because
there is no end or present
other than you: I ask you to hear me.

The Metronome

You started the metronome, Lord,
you only know when,
you only know why. You gave it tension to last,
timing and motion to read.
You stepped out of solitude, Lord.
You timed yourself and us.

You folded rhythm and space
into a perpetual celebration,
spacing its movements and
sounds into eons for the
future to look back and to say:
"The metronome of the Lord is
moving, soon it will strike again."

Life

Tale of a Million Fleas

I opened the door,
I should not have,
but I had a job to do.
I opened the door.
No sooner than that
I closed it, I closed it well.
I only took away what
my eyes picked up
and my ears could not ignore.

The room was empty
except for a creature, a woman
perhaps, sitting on the dingy
floor, covered with rags,
her hair hiding a face
she did not want to show.

A cloud was shielding
her, moving like silent
waves of an ocean, not quite,
it was a little musical
with thousands of notes,
all identical, making some sense.

There was a hum and a vision.
I saw the top of the cloud
changing to the grayish hum
like chanting to get attention.
It was a concert and a
performance of a million fleas
and one spectator in rags.

Before the Big Fall

The crowd moved to the right,
moved to the left, whorled and
cheered and booed and felt
important. There never was
a crowd like this before,
never in a thousand years.

There never was a delusion
like this. Many aching hearts
hoped for the future, facts took
a dive, facts were the losers.
Hopes were riding on trains,
cars, planes, horses and camels.

The blindfolds were neatly in place,
there was air between the ground
and the soles of shoes, boots and sandals.
Walking was easy, there was much
floating, arriving nowhere, just
an attempt to soar before the big fall.

The Plight of the Semicolon

For John Knoepfle

The semicolon rolled
calmly along the highway
separating the docile and
unruly vehicles when
suddenly it lost its head.
What was left was useless.
Shoulders sitting on
an ever slimming sickly
body just wobbling along.
No longer in charge
of anything, not
even itself; without a head
it had no distinction,
no destination, nothing.
It even had a different name.

The Kite

Our kite flew higher and higher
as we released the line. Our
fingers celebrated the wind,
the height, the sheer fact that
our creation sailed
up enough to see the other
side of the granite mountain,
that it did what we never
could. We never climbed
to the top. The kite lifted
us, it gave wings to our
dreams. It served our wishes
and our eyes, supported our
breaths and spoke to the world.
Simple language at the end
of a simple string moving and
aiming and looking down at times.

Special Day

For Randy Holland

Time flies on invisible wings,
in them time finds truth and devotion,
servitude and creation. The wings live.
We know that. Tough we can't see them
we insist that they reveal themselves.
So, we see the Plymouth Rock, the Alamo,
Lewis and Clark, the Oregon and Santa Fe Trails
the birth of the railroad, the first transatlantic flight
and many things closer to home.
Our hearts reach out and celebrate,
get on the wings of time and make discoveries
about things that might go unnoticed.
Things of importance, measurable by
neighborly smiles, sighs and inerasable
realization that time and life go
hand in hand but time goes on
after the hand turns into dust and turns into stone.
That realization takes us to the present.
We should savor it, worship it, and make it holy.
We should celebrate and circle
ourselves and the globe with elation
and invigorating realities of action,
persistency and give ourselves and
the world, like the invisible wing
to time, devotion. We should celebrate.
Yes, every day, but really mostly
on special days, like today.

Contemplation

My polarity is different.
I am between portrait and landscape.
This is not the way to be.
This is a steady state
not moving back and forth.
A mirror half clear and half dull.
Foggy notions leave my chest
about dying, not really just
so far, not frightening just off beat,
as if death were an
exception, happening sometime,
not the rule, not the share
of all of us, not at all, but
an ornamental end of suspended
animation, even glorious.

Without

When you are without,
the leaves fall into
humble piles and dry
out fast. The fingers cannot
find the cord, there is no
harmony. The snow flakes
are all alike, shapelessly white.
Roads end up like snakes
in a basket, birds don't dare
to fly. The thin air will not
support them. Thunder and
lightening and rain and hail
follow your steps and make
you stop, when you are without.

Never Again

I said "never again"
too many times.
"Never again" had a home
right on my shoulders.
It offered aid like a
Good Samaritan.
It served me well,
in retrospect. A preventive
force it never was.
"Never again" was a comfort,
solid and predictable.
It still is.

The Exhibit

The pictures on the wall
looked at us with
critical eyes. They never
blinked, they never missed
a moment nor the vitality
of our eyes and faces.

We looked back and
our senses played a
number of notes, perhaps
out of tune but relevant
and matching and appreciating
of all those framed and alive.

There was a mood and flame
in our hearts in response.
An internal creation
of comfort, understanding,
appreciation and volatility:
The pictures came to us.

A unity of fearless honor,
unmistakable camaraderie
without deception, almost like
never ending understanding with
warm signals from
pictures to bodies, from bodies
to pictures, a composite exhibit.

Talk of the Flowers

When flowers talk to each other
the universe must listen.
Burned out cold planets,
glowing infernos and spaces
built of solid nothing wish
for softness, not seen, felt,
or obtainable where they are.
They listen to feel better.

There is a steady ache among
the planets, shared vastness
of space, an almost absolute coldness,
an ache for beauty, softness
and intimate happiness.
The talk of the spheres drops
to a silence when flowers talk,
wishing for it to last and last.

Words Postponed

I feel as if I should
tell you something, a little
thing, just a short utter
and you would listen.

Then I say nothing. I look
at you and wait. Our
waiting eyes are silent.
We reflect the stillness.

It feels good. Then days pass.
Is it still there what was
unsaid? The impatience is
growing. It takes on

natural dimensions, drives
acts and dreams dressed
in meaning. It is late. Tomorrow,
if I still like you, I tell everything.

The Photographer

For Scott Edwards

You took it upon yourself
to freeze eternity.
Split seconds of time and
your silver emulsion
serve you as your tools
that captivate and capture.
Eternity on display, caged
never to escape. You have
power to shorten eternity,
perhaps even to end it.
It will take you forever.

The Hurt Dimension

The rooms were old in this
old house, older than the walls.
Enclosed spaces next and above
remembered the time before
they were captured by brick and mortar.

It is not the captive air that tries
to escape, it is not the memories
carved and etched and scratched
that hate their prison, it is the
space that longs for freedom.

The infinite, the eternal is hurt
day after day, at times crudely and
violently. Eyes and brains are told
that portioned, parceled and divided
space is our image, the right image.

There was a time, before measured time,
when hands and eyes were useless.
The rooms remember that, the
space, the empty rarified nothing, the
strength and base is hurt and longing.

On the Run

They walked and talked
and hurried. Their hair
kept pace with them, as
they laughed. The times were
good. On time, back
to work.

The table was small,
the plates were large,
pleasing the eyes more
than the stomach.
They swallowed and glanced deeply.
In a hurry again? The sun asked.

There were candles and fine
aromas, waiters and bottles
of wine, music and low-key
whispers, flickering emotions,
watching the clock, hearths in
Throats, a pleasant feeling.

He turned out the light.
They collided, nails worked
and lips burned. High pitch.
The most out of line, the
most out of time and body,
the most on the run.

The Stone Catchers

The stone moved swiftly
toward the moon, propelled by a youthful hand
to tease the bats.

Too many times fooled,
the bats blended
and shimmered, ignored
the bait as it fell.

Are we not like the
bats, baited and let
down, promised and left
alone with nothing to show?

Words and words and words
again are tossed our way.
Words like "I do," "forever" and "always."
Do they ever stay?

Do they float to be captured
treasured and decorated"?
We are the bats of the exploiters.
We have learned not to catch stones.

The Flight

It was one of those yesterdays
that is measured by the flow of years.
I may have been twelve or fourteen perhaps.

The summer arrived, limping a little,
leveling to heat, blessing and peace.
You were my fried, very, very young.

You had feathers and wings very weak.
You followed my steps lest I missed you.
There were you spanning distance and time.

You grew and blossomed and I knew
your time would come and mine too.
The summer would pass, it did, it did.

You walked away one day, I watched you.
The sky looked at you, you looked back.
Both of you knew the meaning well.

You on the ground, your kinfolk in the heights.
You turned, your face was sad.
Then you flew with sure wings
and I cried.

Two Nights, Two Places

The moon looked oval
like a cat's iris in the sunshine.
It was a special night
full of promises, lies and memories.

Few nights turn out that way.
Humble citations from the bible
are more common, silent
jubilations and sighs to please.

Two forms of ecstasy two
houses apart. A distance so
large as to be bridgeable in a few steps
creating two images and slumber.

When the dew lifted from the grass
clothes resumed their usual duty.
Eyes and brains wondered what next?
Both houses found the answer.

The Comet

How many units of
amplified time did it
take to leave your spot in space
and begin to wander?

Galaxies envy you now.
You have a future
and you have a past.
You are in motion,
still burning, still fulfilling
the aim of aims, the law.

You are the purest of all fames.
You are feared and admired.
You must feel good.
You are the neighbor of nobody.
Nobody knocks on your door.
You are on your own.

The Unexpected

Do you see the pictures;
not on the wall,
not in the sky,
not in the turbulent
nothingness, around you
but inside, deep in
your being, painted
fresh, still trying to dry?

Do you hear the sound
galloping, guided by
reins held by hands
unknown, even nonexistent?
It is here, clear and
unobstructed. It will
burst and deliver
a message, unsuspected,
painted and composed.
The unexpected will arrive.

To a Tulip

Why are you open at night?
Can you absorb the darkness
and turn it into color of life?
Temptation told you a thousand times
to fold your petals, bow your
head and wake up one
morning like all the others.
You are different. You absorb,
you convert, you evolve.
You cause pleasure and absolve.
You are the tulip of the night.

Sundown on the Road

The clouds washed
soft grayish lines
in heartwarming tones
over the point where
the road dips away.

Traveling the road
is a pleasure now.
Freedom and space
with wide embrace
temper the speed.

The point keeps moving,
the lines soften
into a colored net of
impatient temperament
before retiring and fade.

The road moans and
stretches and feels lost.
Dark arms offer an
ever stronger embrace.
Now the lines are gone.

Without Awareness

Looking at the wall,
the color changes,
intricate designs appear,
gold mixes in
like an apostolic declaration.
The wall talks.
Deciphering is impossible,
must feel, must intermix,
must communicate, satisfy.
The wall cannot remain
silent. No, it must offer
advice, large and
open, spacious and dire.
The wall breathes,
it whispers and shouts,
all in color in a tone
of mystery. Yet the
message is clear. The message
is storable, not understandable
but useable sometime,
sometime later
without awareness, without awareness.

A Sigh

A sigh stays alive so little,
So little can it say.
Yet, to you it means a lot.

What does it tell that you don't know?
You know it well: It tears your inside
into a breeze like it never lived.
Your past slips by your lips,
no curse, no kiss can tame it.
Your life rides on it.
It faints and fades. You blame it.
You say, I could, I would and alike.

Then you let it die.
One day you'll go down
falling, falling behind a sigh.

Of Song, of Life

Your chanting makes you dead
'cause you don't have a song.
You were born in a courthouse file,
born for the record.

Your lips are a livid,
they can't be taught to sing.
You must be born again for life now.

Start now, start to sing.
Start to hurt before the shadows
team up with your lips
for eternal silence.

For chanting is defeat.
Singing is victory.
Drink it, drink it,
tell the gods you're here.

The Choice

Time looks at us
with questioning eyes.
We look back almost frozen.
We know that we live
in compressed time,
unless we bare our
bodies and souls
and do what we should have
done years ago. The choice
is ours. We can die
now in our frames
or we can have
our frames take on beauty
for others to see,
admire and envy.
We have a choice
before the funeral.

The Outcome

I had to prove the improvable
some time ago.
I tapped into the impossible
to make a point.
I had it coming to me,
So I thought, so I thought.
Alarmist I never was,
failure for me never existed.
It was around, always around,
Lurking, scheming, conniving,
I ignored it, always ignored it.

Ignoring you can only so long.
Something sets in, it chisels
into stone that you don't
want to see, don't want to see.
Look at me now, failure,
look at me now. Who is
the loser, do you know?
If failure wins, it's a loss,
If failure loses, it's a win.
I never thought I'd see them both,
but I have, I sure have.

Gordius

I've never seen the invisible.
The visible has been hiding.
I want to focus once, my eyes
I just want to focus.

I've tried the impossible,
the possible just evaded
all the chances real and unreal,
the possible just evaded.

What is left is dream, obsession
with what is and what is not.
Tomorrow or thereafter
I will dare to cut the knot.

Silence

Silence and solitude, welcome.
No sound, nothing around: a jewel.
For years you knocked on my door.
I kept you out. You tried to prove
the obvious: sound begets sound.
It twists, it twirls,
it wraps you until you suffocate.
It unwraps you naked.
It vibrates around you,
your muscles twitch and ache
because you dare.
It is finished now,
it is silence and solitude
simple and beautiful.

The Laughter of the Storm

The storm pushed hard
against the forest.
Branches fell and roots surfaced,
naked and confused.

Some storms laugh
when they move on.
This one did like
parasites on the kill.

It laughed at the sky
it laughed at the earth
it laughed at the naked
roots on the ground.

Have you heard the
laughter of the storm?
A neighbor asked.
I nodded. At the distance
I still heard the thunder.

Back, Back, Way Back

We stood there in front of the temple.
The marble gleamed against the blue.
Clouds of crows swirled in the sky,
hoping to die.

We stood there alive, looking for more
years to come, more years to live,
more years to love, more of all this
never to die.

We stood there frozen, just like the temple,
we gleamed, I think, ignoring the crows.
They fell in black heaps. We never moved,
just stared at the sky.

Lament to a Dove

There are no olive branches
around here my dove.
There is no peace either,
as you know,
just thistles and thorns.

Where is your freedom?
Your flight is hampered,
your aim is trimmed
like your wings, 'cause
thistles and thorns
don't usher in peace.

At the End of the Road

There is something at the end of the road.
I can see it.
Waving, waiting, breathing.
There is something.
I must go there,
I must see, I must feel,
I must wave back,
shake hands
Or just admire,
just be there.
Because there is something,
only the road has no end,
it never ends.

There is something at the end of the road,
day in, day out,
just waiting.
Lights come and go,
waves freeze, then break and crack.
I am on my way.
There, where the light freezes,
where the blue is silver,
at the end of the road
that never ends.
I must go there some day.

Books by Pearn and Associates, Inc.

Mathematics in Color, Joseph J. Kozma (poetry)

Black 14, Ryan Thorburn (nonfiction)

Walking in Snow, John Knoepfle (poetry)

A Lenten Journey Towards Christian Maturity,
  Father William E. Breslin (a prayer guide)

I Look Around for my Life, John Knoepfle
  (autobiography)

Ikaria: A Love Odyssey on a Greek Island,
  Anita Sullivan (nonfiction)

The U Book, Nathan Pierce (photography)

Another Chance, Joe Naiman, (fiction)

Goulash and Picking Pickles, Louise Hoffmann
  (autobiography)

Point Guard, Victor Pearn (fiction)

Printed in the United States
215904BV00001B/17/P